Factories, Forges and Foundries

Factories, Forges and Foundries

Industrial buildings of Britain

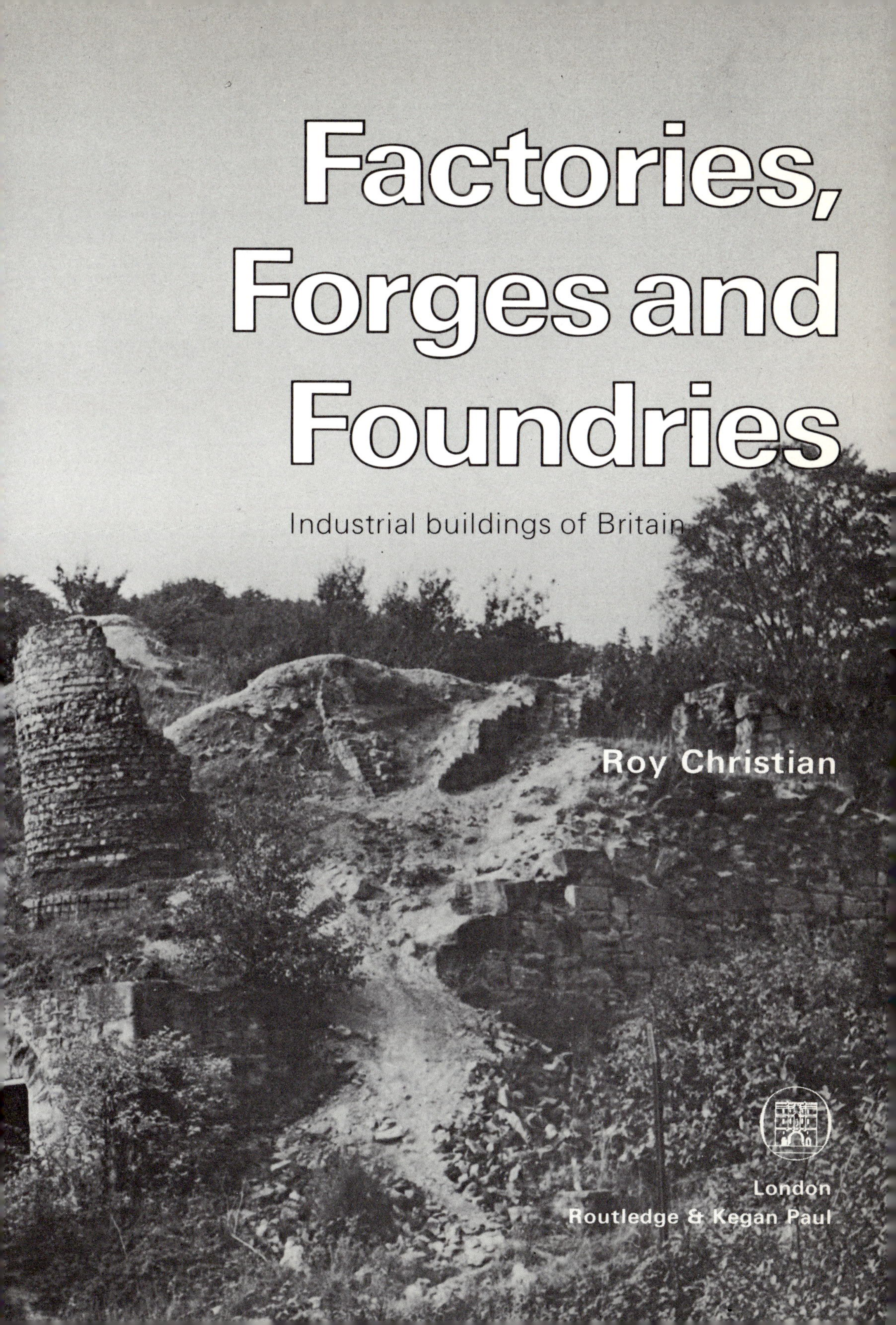

Roy Christian

London
Routledge & Kegan Paul

First published in 1974
by Routledge & Kegan Paul Ltd
Broadway House, 68–74 Carter Lane,
London EC4V 5EL
Filmset and printed in Great Britain by
BAS Printers Limited, Wallop, Hampshire

ISBN 0 7100 7901 X

Photographs by Frank Rodgers

Frontispiece: *Ruined lime kilns at Bull Bridge in Derbyshire. The kilns were built towards the end of the eighteenth century and remained in use until about 1930.*

Contents

'. . . all the business of life is to endeavour to find out what you don't know by what you do'

John Whiting *Marching Song*

Editor's preface

Until about two hundred years ago most things were made by hand, but nowadays nearly everything we use is made by people working in industry. The buildings in which the work is done have changed a great deal; there are fashions in factories, forges, foundries and warehouses, just as there are in houses, schools, churches and shops. And fashions are always interesting because they tell us about *people*, what they do and what they try to do at any particular time.

This book is to help you to enjoy looking at buildings which you may never have noticed before, and to understand their importance. If you are planning to do a project on industrial buildings you will have to use your eyes and your imagination. You will need to talk to local people and keep your eye on the local paper, to find out how things have changed and whether there are any plans for the future. You will have to decide how you are going to present your work and how you are going to divide it up. You might be interested to study a single building or a group of buildings, perhaps buildings concerned with a particular branch of industry, or even all the industrial buildings in your town, though that might be very difficult.

Remember how important *looks* are in anything we do. However original and interesting your notes or charts may be, however pleasing and accurate your drawings, models and photographs, they will not really attract anybody unless your work is tidy, your captions clear and your headings well-spaced. Tape recordings, too, need to have titles and other information on a label.

Perhaps you have thought of industrial buildings as just 'work places', and indeed that is what they are. But when you have read this book you may begin to see that there is history there too, fine architecture sometimes, and painting, design and literature. There are clues and interests and pleasures to be found everywhere if we look carefully.

M.H.

Looking around

1

Finding out about local industry

Large and small firms

Who owns them

The look of the buildings

'Industry' used to mean 'cleverness' and we still describe somebody as 'industrious' when they are hard-working. It was not until the eighteenth century, when steam power was developed, that 'industry' came to mean what it does today – work done in factories, forges, foundries, mills, quarries, mines and so on. But of course there were work-places like that long before the new word came to be used.

Industrial work produces most of the things we all use, yet it is only very recently that people have started to be interested in the history of industrial buildings. So there are still a lot of things to be found out – about old or ruined buildings, about strange lumps in the ground in places where buildings may once have stood, about peculiar names on a map, or interesting local legends. Maps can be particularly useful. Village names like New Invention in Shropshire and Ironville in Derbyshire suggest that these were villages built round a works. Field-names on maps can be interesting too, and so can signs indicating a disused windmill, or a disused tramway that probably once led to a works. You could perhaps start your project from some small clue like that.

Where to begin?

It is a good idea to look first at your own home town or village. Is it a place where most people work in factories or mines or on the land? You may think yours is a sleepy village with no industry. But are you sure? Think about the man round the corner who

Electric power station, Ratcliffe-on-Soar, Nottinghamshire. The cooling towers on the left were unfinished when the photograph was taken.

repairs car bodies. He runs an industry even though he may employ only another man and a boy. So do look closely.

If you live in a big town, like Blackburn or Rotherham, you will see by the factories, mills and mines that it is industrial. But do you know how many industries there are in the town? Be careful about this. You need not bother yet about the number of separate works. Just consider how many different kinds of goods are produced in the town.

If you live in Oxford or Coventry you will know that motor car manufacturing is your most important industry. As well as firms that assemble the cars, there are others making parts for them. But there are other industries not connected with motor cars. See if you can find out what they are.

Finding out about local industry

One way of finding out about local industry is to walk round the town and count the number of separate works. This will teach you a lot about your town, but it may take a long time.

It is quicker to consult the local telephone directory which will have classified trade sections at the back – printed on yellow paper. They will list separate firms under such headings as Paint Manufacturers, Toolmakers, Watch and Clock Makers and so on. Your public library may also have street directories of the town going back to about 1830. These will help you to trace the industrial history of the town; you can find out from old directories how long a firm has been established there.

You may discover that there have been changes in the type of industry. Derby, for instance, had fourteen silk mills a century or so ago; today there are none. It would be interesting to find out the reasons for such a startling change.

The range of industries

You may be surprised at the number of different industries and works you discover. Even without its silk mills, Derby has more than a hundred different industries and many hundred individual firms. Other towns of similar size have far fewer; Stafford for example relies heavily on electrical engineering; Barrow-in-Furness could not survive without ship-building. Think out whether it is better for a town to have a wide variety of industries or to concentrate on one or two. If you live in South Wales or County Durham you will have seen the distress caused when coal mines close, and you will have no doubt about your answer. You can read a vivid account of life in Jarrow when its ship-building yards closed in *English Journey* by J. B. Priestley.

Other reasons for preferring a town to have a variety of industries may occur to you. What about jobs to choose from when you leave school?

Large and small firms

Let us now take a closer look at your town's industries. Are they mainly big firms employing several thousand people, or small

The Weavers, a group of Tudor houses overlooking the River Stour, Canterbury. In the upper storey there are old looms, brought over by Flemish and French refugees, and exhibitions of weaving can be seen.

ones with just a few workers? In the Staffordshire Black Country there are some big works, but most are quite small. In workshops little bigger than cowsheds a few men will be busy making chains or anchors. Birmingham also has many small workshops. This is the way that industry started in the West Midlands and it is slow to change.

Sheffield's industry, on the other hand, has altered a great deal. Its iron and steel industry grew up in a lot of small works, often with the workmen's cottages close by. These formed almost separate villages inside the town.

A complete eighteenth-century works of this kind has been preserved in Sheffield as an industrial museum. This 'Abbeydale Industrial Hamlet' is well worth visiting. There – at certain times of the day – you can see four water wheels, powered by the fast flowing River Sheaf, turning to drive the machinery that once made scythes and sickles. Today such small foundries are rare, and most people there work in large steel works. It is worth considering why this kind of change has happened in so many places.

Ownership of industry

Nowadays much of our industry is owned by a few big firms. Is this the case in your town? Are there local men in charge, or are the works part of a big organization with branches elsewhere?

If you are keen on football, you may have noticed that it is usually the big city clubs – Manchester, Liverpool, London, Leeds and Glasgow – that win most of the trophies. This is largely because these clubs can draw big crowds from where a lot of people live. They use the gate money to enlarge their grounds to hold still more people, pay high transfer fees for good players and high wages to keep them.

Much the same happens in industry. The bigger firms can afford to pay high wages for good workmen, buy the best machinery and get their raw materials cheaper by buying them in large quantities. The smaller firms find it difficult to compete. So the trend is for them to be bought out by larger firms, which, then,

Abbeydale Industrial Hamlet, Sheffield, where scythes and sickles were first made in the eighteenth century. Now it is an industrial museum, open daily.

of course, become larger still. You may have noticed that motor cars are now manufactured by a few giant firms, and that most of our chemicals are produced by the vast Imperial Chemicals Industry. A lot of capital is now required to run a business. (Look up that word *capital* – you might find it worthwhile to discuss it with your economics teacher. Find out too what is meant by a *take over*.)

These changes in the ownership of industry should mean that goods can be produced and sold more cheaply and efficiently, but sometimes the opposite happens and the prices rise because of lack of competition, and there are fewer jobs about.

The type of northern industrial scene that L. S. Lowry paints. This one is Derby, and most of these buildings date from the nineteenth century. How many different kinds of building materials can you spot?

Raw materials

Raw materials are the basic elements from which things are manufactured; coal, iron ore, timber and copper are some of them.

Do you know where your local firms get their raw materials? There is a disused ironworks near my home which obtained all of its raw materials – including the materials from which the works was built – from within a ten-mile radius. This kept transport costs low, but nowadays many firms have to bring their raw materials from widely scattered parts of the world. It would be interesting to know just where your local firms get their materials and how they are transported. You could show this on a map.

How would you find out about these sources of raw materials? Perhaps if you are concerned with a small firm and know somebody working there you might get all your information just by asking.

For a bigger firm or firms it might be better to write a letter explaining what you want to know and why. If several of you are working on the same project, one letter will do – this will save the firm time and money, and is much more likely to bring you an answer. Remember to write a brief 'thank you' letter.

If you are lucky you may receive pamphlets giving information about the firm's history and details of its present work. If they are illustrated some of the pictures could be stuck into your booklet or onto a group chart.

The appearance of buildings

Notice what the industrial buildings in your town look like. They may be old-fashioned foundries, belching out smoke, or equally old-fashioned textile mills, tall, bare, sooty and ugly. A Lancashire artist, L. S. Lowry, has painted some wonderful pictures of industrial scenes like these. They are well worth finding, and you might like to include a postcard of a Lowry painting in your project.

But your local industrial buildings may be more modern: 'glittering white structures of concrete, glass and steel, surrounded by green lawns and beds of tulips', as George Orwell described them in *The Road to Wigan Pier.* Your English teacher might read you extracts from this book, which gives an accurate but depressing picture of industry as it was forty years ago.

If your project is on one particular industrial building it is important to describe its appearance accurately. Draw a picture of it, or make a model, or you could take several photographs from different positions, getting the firm's permission first. A plan would be interesting, if you are allowed inside.

Even if you are writing about the industries of a whole town it is still a good idea to describe one typical building. It is even more important to draw a sketch-map showing the position of the main works. If you are dealing with a large town, do not put in *every* building; that would be tedious and would make the map look cramped. When you have drawn the map, several questions may occur to you, but these can be left to a later chapter.

2

The placing of industrial buildings

Choosing an industrial site

Proximity of raw materials

People, power and communications

Planning

When you go camping you are unlikely just to stop when you feel tired and pitch your tent wherever you happen to be. You probably think carefully before choosing a site.

You will select level ground rather than lumpy turf or a steep hill-side, and you will look for a stream to supply water for cooking and washing, but you will avoid marshy ground. If the weather is bad you may search for a sheltered position, and you may like to be near a farm so that you can get milk.

Choosing an industrial site

Industrialists have to think in much the same way when they choose a site for their works. Like you, they do not just pick the first vacant piece of land they find, though it is true that some industries have little choice. For instance, coal mines have to be sunk where there is coal and quarries must be worked where there is stone.

Raw materials

Manufacturing industries have more freedom of choice, though they have to think carefully about costs and about getting their raw materials. Coal and iron are expensive to move, so iron and steel works are usually close to coalfields or iron-ore beds.

The discovery of iron-ore in the Cleveland Hills in the early nineteenth century brought the iron and steel industry to nearby

Teesside. Middlesbrough, which had previously been a small village, developed rapidly into a large town and the centre of the industry. Much the same thing happened in many other places.

If you ever travel to London from the North, you will see the tall chimneys of brickworks in Bedfordshire, apparently in the heart of the country. It seems strange until you notice that the clay for making bricks is dug out of the ground nearby.

Raw materials are not always close at hand. If they have to be imported it is important for the factory to be near a port, and this is equally essential for exporting goods. One reason why the cotton industry settled in Lancashire was that Liverpool was able to handle the raw cotton from the USA.

Often, though, the reasons for the location of a particular industry are less obvious. Have you ever wondered, for instance, why Burton-on-Trent became famous for brewing? Its secret lies buried underground. The town's water supply comes from springs in the Trent Valley that pass between layers of a rock called gypsum which gives a flavour that is considered ideal for brewing. It would be interesting to find other examples where nature has provided a town with its livelihood.

Modern brickworks, Bedfordshire. The bricks are made from local clay. Why are there so many chimneys, and why are they so tall?

Tradition

Tradition may also influence the choice of an industrial site, for example in areas where people have learnt ways of doing certain types of work. Leicester people are used to dealing with textiles, which was the reason given by one firm recently for starting a new textile factory there. Similarly, a new firm wanting to make china would be likely to settle in the Potteries because there are many skilled potters in that area.

Light industries – those not producing heavy goods or handling bulky materials – are often less concerned about where a factory should be built. Sometimes the choice will depend on some fairly small point: for example, Rolls-Royce hesitated whether to build their motor-car works at Derby or Leicester and finally chose Derby because electricity there was cheaper.

Labour

It is not much use building a factory in an isolated area where there are no people. Houses have to be built and workers have to be offered high wages and what are called 'fringe benefits' to tempt them to move. Ask your father what kind of benefits these are. They have probably changed since 1787 when a cotton-spinning firm called Evans and Sons opened a new mill at Darley Abbey near Derby and advertised in newspapers that they would build houses for the workers and provide a cow free for each family. The cow idea was a good one, for in those days of low wages many families had very little money to spend on milk. If you look at the job advertisements in newspapers you will see various benefits offered to employees.

Power and communications

Early industry needed water-power to drive machinery, and often a river was needed for carrying goods in days when roads were bad. Yet too much water could cause havoc. So usually the old factories stood fairly high above normal flood dangers. It would be a good idea to look at the map of your local industries and see how many are still situated alongside a river or stream.

Flooding and drought were among the reasons that made early

Darley Abbey Mill, Derby, was a textile mill from 1783 to 1970. Until 1968 it was powered by water. These early nineteenth-century buildings are still in use for industry.

industrialists think of better forms of transport. Canals, first cut in the 1760s, solved some of the problems. They provided a fairly reliable form of transport, which was safe for breakable goods. That is why Josiah Wedgwood decided to build a new pottery alongside the Trent and Mersey Canal at Etruria. Colliery owners, whose mines were often far from a river, were able to send coal more cheaply and further by using canals. The canal that cuts through your town may not be much used now, but you will probably still find works along its banks. You can be sure that they were built in the eighteenth or early nineteenth centuries and the locks will have been installed then.

Canal transport was slow and by about 1850 much of the trade had been lost to railways. You can still see old works alongside the railway lines and at the approaches to almost any large station. Most of them will have been there for a century or more.

Nowadays much more than half our goods are carried by lorry, and so many modern factories are situated alongside main roads on the outskirts of cities. Whether this is a good thing is something else that you could usefully discuss in class. Think about road safety and the risk of spoiling the appearance of a city;

about the dangers likely to be caused by even bigger container lorries and whether more use might be made of the railways and canals.

If your project deals with your own town it would be useful to draw small sketch-maps of the rivers, canals, railway lines and roads, indicating the position of each factory alongside them by a cross or a small drawing.

You should also find out the exact dates when the canal and railway reached your town, and how soon after the factories alongside them were built. Many rivers were dredged and widened between 1620 and 1760 to make them navigable. It would be interesting to find out if that happened to your river and if any works were built along its banks.

You will now see the importance of communications in the siting of industry and how the transport of goods has changed over the years. What changes are likely in the future? If there is an airport near your town it would be worthwhile looking if any works have been built nearby and whether they are connected with the aircraft industry, or if they make use of air transport.

Beauty and the Beast. A cement works at Hope, in the Peak National Park, scars a lovely countryside.

Perhaps you live in a district where it is planned to build a new airport or motorway. If so you could conduct an interesting survey by asking local people what they think of the idea.

You may find that shopkeepers, local councillors and the unemployed want the airport because it could result in more trade and jobs, but that most others are against it. They may fear increased noise from aircraft, the loss of farming land, the spoiling of an attractive stretch of countryside, the disturbance of wild life, and above all, the demolition of their homes, and perhaps of entire villages.

The fact is that while many people want new airports few want them near their own homes. Much the same thing applies to new motorways. So here again, you have a good topic for class discussion. In a thickly-populated island, how much land – and how many amenities – can we sacrifice for large civil engineering projects?

Power stations

In recent years many electric power stations have been built on river banks, so that rivers supply power as they did centuries ago,

Sometimes industry fits into beautiful surroundings; this hosiery mill at Bonsall, Derbyshire, is screened by trees and rising ground. The mill is built by a stream that once provided its power.

though in a different way.

If you draw a map of all the power stations along the Trent, Severn or Thames, you will see this. The power generated along the Trent may light up houses in Slough or Reading a hundred miles away. Have you ever asked where your power supply comes from? It may reach you through the National Grid system and a polite letter to the Central Electricity Generating Board could bring some interesting information about this.

This disused stretch of the Derby Canal (opened in 1792) has now been drained and lies under a new road. The centre buildings have been demolished, but the others remain – the one on the extreme right was a salt warehouse built in 1820. Notice the hoist and the rotting boat below.

If there is a power station near you, you could find out where its coal comes from and whether it is carried by railway, road or river. It would be interesting to know how the power stations dispose of their ash and other waste materials. Another important question is whether it is better to have a power station near a river or near a coal mine.

This tilt-hammer at Abbeydale was made in about 1790 but is still working daily. Its massive main shaft is made of oak, and is driven by the water-wheel, 18 feet in diameter.

Nuclear power stations

Not all modern power stations use coal or are sited near rivers. Nuclear power stations are more likely to be situated on the coast, like those at Sizewell in Suffolk and near Amlwch in Anglesey. If you find out how such power stations work and which raw materials are used you could discuss their advantages and disadvantages.

Development areas

Nowadays governments try to encourage firms to move to areas such as County Durham and South Wales where pit closures have caused much unemployment, or to rather isolated areas such as Cornwall and the Scottish islands where there is little work in the winter when the holiday makers have gone home. The managers of a firm who want to build a new factory in one of these 'Development Areas' can ask the Government for a grant of money which will cover much of the cost of building.

You probably know whether yours is a Development Area or whether there is enough work available. The local newspapers usually give the number of people unemployed in the area each month. You could draw a graph showing how unemployment has risen and fallen over a period and try to explain the causes.

National Parks

Since 1949 ten areas of great natural beauty in Great Britain have been declared National Parks. The few industries already in these areas, such as quarrying in the Peak District and Snowdonia, were allowed to continue, but new 'heavy' industries were not encouraged. When mining companies wanted to search for minerals – potash in the North Yorkshire Moors, copper in Snowdonia – there was a public outcry. Yet there are people out of work in these areas and many local people are in favour of allowing some industries to develop there. A class discussion about these opposite points of view would be interesting.

Planning restrictions

As we have seen from the National Parks, the days when an industrialist could build his works just where he wished are over. Round most towns there are 'green belts' of countryside which can only be built over in exceptional circumstances.

Nowadays nobody is allowed to build a house – or put even a new porch to an existing house – without getting 'planning permission' from the local authority. The same thing applies to industrial buildings. If permission to build is given it will probably be in a part of the town away from residential areas.

Look at the map of your town and see whether most heavy industries are on the east side. Try to work out why this is. Think of the direction of the wind and what unpleasantness it can cause if you live in the lee of a factory. If you have a wind gauge at school you might check the number of days in the year when the wind blows from a westerly direction.

Industrial archaeology 3

Looking for early industrial buildings

Clues in names

Clues from photography

Old mines and railways

River and canal buildings

Industry in Britain is very old and some of the most interesting early industrial buildings are those you cannot see. This may sound strange, but it is true – they are hidden underground and in order to see them people have to dig. It is only quite recently that people have become interested in the relics of early industry and have given the name industrial archaeology to this fascinating study.

The Romans worked lead mines in the Mendips in Somerset and the Derbyshire Peak nearly 2,000 years ago and they mined tin in Cornwall. Most Roman industrial buildings have gone, but occasionally traces of them are dug up. If you go to the Roman villa at Chedworth in Gloucestershire you will see a building in which cloth was produced in the days when Britain was the western outpost of the Roman Empire. Near Duffield in Derbyshire, large quantities of Roman pottery have been found. When local archaeologists obtained permission to dig in a field where pieces of pot had been turned up by the plough, they also found the remains of a Roman pottery kiln. That kiln had been out of use for nearly 1,600 years.

Looking for early industrial buildings

Industrial buildings of a much later date have for a long time been buried and forgotten. An engineer who spent much of his childhood with an aunt at a farmhouse called Furnace Farm often played in a field that contained many strange humps. These meant little to him then, but years later, on hearing that the farm was to be drowned under a new reservoir, he obtained permission to dig there. Helped by a few friends, he spent several weekends before unearthing the remains of a stone furnace in which iron had been smelted.

Later research in libraries proved that there had been an iron-works on the Furnace Farm site until the early eighteenth century, when part of it must have been demolished. The rest soon became hidden under grass and scrub until only the humps and the name – Furnace Farm – remained as clues that it ever existed.

Sometimes a pond may be the only trace of a disused iron-works. These ponds, called hammer ponds, were formed by damming a stream. Water was allowed to fall through a sort of movable shutter, called a sluice, at the lower end of the pond. This water worked the bellows to provide a blast for the furnace and turned a wheel which operated a hammer for beating iron into sheets.

The hammer pond at Abbeydale is now an ornamental lake in a public park. Another gave its name to the Surrey village of Abinger Hammer, not far from that lovely expanse of water at Friday Street that served the same purpose in the days when Surrey, Sussex and Kent were centres of the iron industry.

If you come across traces of what you think may be an early industrial site it would be worth mentioning them to your history teacher, who would put you in touch with people interested in industrial archaeology. You could be the first person to have noticed the site. If so, you should certainly report it to the National Record of Industrial Monuments, Bath University of Technology, Bath, Somerset.

Clues in names

Just as Abinger Hammer reveals the name of an ancient village industry, so street names sometimes give clues to the position of old works. Foundry Lane, Forge Row, Furnace Terrace and Cinder Hill are all street names I know which appeared meaning-

less until I discovered that they marked the sites of former ironworks. Perhaps you can find similar road names in your district.

Street names and inn-signs are often valuable clues to former industrial sites. The Lime Kiln Inn at Breedon-on-the-Hill, Leicestershire, stands close to a large limestone quarry.

Often the clue is less obvious. Derby has streets called Handyside Street and Buchanan Street. The names convey nothing unless you happen to know that the streets cover the site of what was once a large engineering works called Handysides, which was managed for a long time by a man called Buchanan. The works closed down suddenly in 1911 and now only the street names indicate the site.

There are clues, too, in inn signs (see the picture above, right) and in farm and field names. By a tiny stream in an isolated stretch of Derbyshire countryside are two fields called Foundry Meadow and Black Pasture. When I asked the landowner about these puzzling names, he showed me documents proving there had once been an ironworks in this remote spot. It was powered by the stream that must then have been deeper and less sluggish. Black Pasture got its name from the now buried heaps of slag, which is the refuse that is left when iron has been smelted (like ashes after a fire). This slag still turns the stream black after heavy rain.

Look up old maps of your district for clues of early industry. Tithe maps, giving field-names, were drawn up for most villages in the late 1830s. Large scale Ordnance Survey maps first appeared about ten years later. Your local library or county records office should have these and other early maps, and some may still be stored in the parish chest, in the church. Your vicar could tell you if there are any maps in his possession.

Clues from photographs

A Leicestershire farmer not long ago noticed that one corner of a cornfield yielded a poorer crop than the rest of the field. He could not account for this, until a friend took photographs from the air and these showed a dark shadow in that corner of the field. This prompted another friend, who was an archaeologist, to dig there after the harvest, and his excavations soon exposed the foundations of buildings that had once stood there.

These proved to be the remains of a small village that had been abandoned in the Middle Ages when arable farming gave way to sheep farming in many parts of England; but they might have been industrial buildings. Aerial photographs can show traces of industrial sites that might otherwise have been forgotten. Pilots see much more below than we do at ground level.

It may not be possible for you to go up in an aeroplane to look for industrial sites, but it is worth your while to examine aerial photographs. Exhibitions of them may sometimes be on view in your local museum. Even if you cannot get hold of aerial photographs easily, you could take shots of the surrounding countryside from a hill-top. These may show traces of industrial relics – especially old mine workings – that are not easy to see lower down.

Old mines

If you live in Derbyshire, Somerset or near the Yorkshire Dales

Entrance to a disused lead mine in Derbyshire. Take great care when exploring lead mining country, for old mine shafts are often deep and dangerous.

you will find much evidence of old lead mine workings. In Cornwall there are relics of ancient tin mining as well as some modern workings. The fields in these areas are often riddled with humps and hollows where the ore has been extracted.

But DO BE CAREFUL. Examining such workings can be dangerous. Some old mines have been filled with earth, others remain open with perhaps a flimsy fence for protection. People, as well as animals, have been killed by falling down old shafts.

Sometimes you may find more than humps and hollows. Occasionally the mine buildings still stand. Cornwall still has old pumping houses (like the one on page 24) and there are buildings standing at the old copper mines at Ecton in the Manifold Valley in Staffordshire.

It is a good idea to take a tape measure with you when you visit these old buildings. Yours could be the only record of their size and appearance, and it could be of historical value should the buildings be demolished. You should also notice if they are of stone and try to identify the type of stone, which is likely to have been quarried nearby. Lead mine buildings will probably be made of limestone; those at the tin mines of granite, though the upper part of the engine-house chimneys may be of brick. You will find *The Observer's Book of Geology* useful in this study.

What I have said about these mines applies also to iron-ore mines and, especially, to coal mines because many have only recently been abandoned and their buildings may still be standing. There may be spoil-heaps, or tips, formed by waste material from the pits, though there are many people who want these levelled, and in some areas this is being done.

Finding the history

Because in the past local history books often ignored industry, it may be difficult to find out the history of these mines. The best source of information could be local people. If you can find a man who worked down a mine he may give you a fascinating story of conditions in his time. If you have a tape recorder you could tape his story in full. If not, use a notebook and jot down the most important points. Have some questions prepared, but be ready to follow up with others if necessary.

The ruined pumping engine house of a disused Cornish tin mine. It is made of the local granite and is tall enough to house a lofty beam engine.

Another beam engine, used to keep the mine clear of water, was housed in this engine house at the Magpie Mine, Sheldon, Derbyshire.

There are many customs, legends and traditions connected with mining, particularly with lead and tin mines. There are also curious technical terms, some in use before the Norman Conquest. You should collect these; they will give life to your project, as will any songs that originated down the mines. You may know 'The Keel Row', which is concerned with the shipment of coal from Tyneside. 'Blaydon Races' is another song closely linked with coal mining.

Disused railways

While investigating disused mines look for traces of abandoned railway tracks. A pair of hedges only a few yards apart may be the only evidence of a narrow-gauge line built a century or two ago as in the picture on page 26.

These railways – sometimes called tramways, or gangways – often linked a mine with the nearest river or canal. On Tyneside the wagon trains were often worked by gravity. Loaded trucks

This track through a wood marks an abandoned railway line that once carried stone from Ticknall, Derbyshire to the Ashby Canal, Leicestershire. Some of the sleepers still remain, almost hidden under grass.

ran downhill and pulled empty trucks uphill by means of an endless chain.

Elsewhere horses pulled the trucks, but a stationary engine would be used for steep gradients. An octagonal engine-house at the top of the 1 in 8 Middleton Incline on the Cromford and High Peak Railway in Derbyshire still houses a beam-engine (see chapter 6) built in 1825. This was used until 1963 to pull truck-loads of stone from local quarries.

By these disused railways you can often find interesting insects and plants. A 360-yard stretch in Huntingdonshire, that has now become a nature reserve, is the home of many unusual plants, at least seventeen species of butterflies and more than two hundred different species of moths. If you know of a disused line it might be worth identifying and listing all the plants you find growing there. But please do not pick any, for they may be very rare.

River and canal ports

If you follow a disused railway track you may well come to a once busy canal or river port. Some old river ports, like Bewdley, on the

Severn, or Bawtry, on the Idle, have only a few old warehouses left, though you can sometimes find an odd one that has been converted to other uses. The best known example is the Maltings, at Snape, by the River Alde in Suffolk. Sea-going steam and sailing barges were unloading American barley there until the Second World War, but then local grown barley was used and brought by lorry. The Maltings closed in 1965 and was converted into a fine concert hall, which was unfortunately badly damaged by fire in 1969. Since then it has been rebuilt, and concerts are broadcast from there during the annual Aldeburgh Festival.

Canal ports, such as Stourport in Worcestershire, West Stockwith in Nottinghamshire, and Shardlow in Derbyshire, have attractive eighteenth- or early nineteenth-century buildings still standing. One large warehouse at Shardlow was built partly over the water and had little tunnels into which the boats could be hauled to load or unload directly under the building.

Canal architects normally used brick for their buildings. Often the clay was dug and baked locally, so look out for abandoned brickyards. Brick waste and shallow clay pits, often overgrown with blackthorn, are clues to look for. You may find such brickyards anywhere in the country, not simply near canal ports.

Morewellham

While we are thinking of inland ports, you might try to find out something about Morewellham. It was once an important river port in Devon, and the busiest copper port in the world in Victorian times. When the trade declined the port was abandoned and almost forgotten. Then in 1970 a large number of volunteers, mainly young people, began to clear away the lush vegetation and expose the old port to public view as a natural, living museum. This was a wonderfully interesting and valuable project. Is there anything similar that you could do in your area?

Seaports

Rivers must eventually go to the sea. If you live near the sea you will find plenty of industrial buildings to look at. Even quite small coastal villages once had flourishing harbours. Blakeney,

Cley and Wells-next-the-Sea, close together on the Norfolk coast, were busy ports in sailing ship days. You will have to look hard at Cley and Blakeney to find the old warehouses, because they are now used for other purposes, but at Wells (see page opposite) they are much easier to recognize.

The bigger ports are changing rapidly. Old buildings are being demolished, new ones put up. Now is the time to examine and record the old ones before it is too late. This is particularly true of London, where the port is being extended towards Tilbury and the old docks are being converted to new uses. All sorts of interesting plans are being discussed, especially for St Katharine's Dock, which is next to the Tower of London and has some splendid old buildings that are being converted into flats, artists' studios and other uses. How are such changes likely to alter our industrial neighbourhood?

A modern grain storage warehouse on the quay at Wells-next-the-Sea, Norfolk. Some of the other buildings may once have been warehouses when this was an important port.

4 Early mills

Water-mills

Mill-wheels

Windmills

Unusual mills

Water-mills

The oldest industrial buildings you are likely to find are water-mills. Archaeologists have found traces of Roman water-mills in various parts of Britain, but after the Romans left people forgot how to use them until the Anglo-Saxons re-introduced them in the eighth century AD. Nearly 6,000 water-mills for grinding corn were mentioned in Domesday Book in 1085–6. A century or so later nearly every village had one, and some larger places had five or six.

Domesday Book was written in Latin, but the *Victoria County History* of your county will have an English translation that you can see in your local library. If your village is mentioned, look if there is reference to a mill.

If there is – or if you can find mention elsewhere of a later water-mill – you might try to find out where it stood. It must have been by a stream, though in a town this may now run underground in a culvert, or large pipe. A street name – Mill Lane or Mill Street – may be a clue, though this could refer to a later type of mill. Old maps in the library may help.

In a village you may be lucky enough to find the mill still standing. It will not be the building mentioned in Domesday Book, but it may stand on the same site. It might even still be working. A few have continued in use for centuries and others have been preserved for people to see. There is a working water-mill in the Castle Museum at York, and others in various museums elsewhere.

This old water-wheel by the River Trent, at Kings Mills near Castle Donington, Leicestershire, is still preserved although not in its original position.

Some old mills have been converted for different uses. Several have become private houses; others cafés. So look carefully at any fairly large building overlooking a stream in case it may once have been a mill. A small cabin sticking out over the water near the top of the building is a sure sign that it was once a mill. The cabin is called a 'lucomb', and was used for unloading grain and loading flour.

Even if the mill building has gone, you may still be able to guess where it stood. Look for a narrow channel of water that has been cut from a main stream. This may be a leat. Along it, water diverted from the main stream would flow quickly to turn the mill-wheel.

Mill-wheels

You may be lucky enough to find a mill-wheel still in position. If not, look for a circular mark on a building close to the water where a wheel may have rubbed against the masonry.

There were three types of water-wheels:
(a) *undershot*, where the water turned the wheel by hitting the

float-boards near the bottom;
(b) *overshot*, where the water ran on to the top of the wheel into 'buckets' on the rim that became heavy enough to start the wheel turning;
(c) *breast*, where the water hit the wheel at about the level of the axle.

You could try to work out for yourself which was the most efficient system. It may be useful to start by considering that an *overshot* wheel would be effective in hilly country where the streams were swift.

Millers

The miller was often mentioned in old stories, poems and songs, and you might find it interesting to look out for such references. Sometimes he is referred to as a 'jolly miller', but more often he was unpopular. Can you suggest possible reasons for this?

Painting of mills

Water-mills often figure prominently in paintings, because they were usually attractive buildings. The best known is Flatford Mill in Suffolk, which was often painted by John Constable, who was born in the mill house. You may like to build up a collection of post-card reproductions of water-mill paintings.

Windmills

Windmills are usually even more attractive than water-mills. Somebody once said: 'Next to ships, windmills are the most beautiful objects that man has built purely for his own use.' That is an idea worth discussing.

Windmills were first used in Arabia, where water was scarce. There is no record of one in Europe before the 1180s, and the first English windmill that we know of was standing at Bury St Edmunds in 1191. After that they became as numerous as water-mills, especially east of a line between the rivers Severn and Trent. Look at a map and try to work out why they were so

Tower-mill at Burgh-le-Marsh, Lincolnshire. It was built about 1833, but still works, and is open to the public. Notice the wooden cap, and attached to it the fantail, ensuring that the sails always face the wind.

common in the eastern counties that a writer named William Cobbett wrote in *Rural Rides* that standing in one spot near Ipswich in 1830 he could see the sails of seventeen windmills all turning at the same time.

Twenty years ago it might have been difficult to find seventeen windmills still working in the whole of Britain, but since then many have been put back into working order. Now almost every county has at least one windmill in working order and which is open to the public. You should try to visit one, and you might be able to do more than that.

The two hundred year-old Cat-and-Fiddle windmill, Dale Abbey, is the only post-mill in Derbyshire still in working order. The beam used for turning the mill into the wind is just visible behind the ladder.

When the Lindsey County Council bought and restored the tower-mill at Burgh-le-Marsh (see picture on page 33) the pupils of William Morris School, Skegness, undertook to clean and paint the inside of the mill and label the machinery. Then they made models of other Lincolnshire windmills, drew maps and copied old documents relating to mills. They displayed these in one of the mil! buildings which is now a local history museum. It might be worth looking around locally to see if you could help with some useful and interesting project like that.

There are three main types of windmills:
(a) *Post-mills* – the earliest kind of windmill – where the whole body of the mill revolves in the wind around a 'main-post' of oak. The bottom part of the main-post may be encased in a round house – probably brick-built – which does not revolve.
(b) *Tower-mills* – which were introduced into England in the fifteenth century. They are usually built of brick or stone and only the cap and the sails attached to it revolve.
(c) *Smock-mills* – introduced about 1650. They are fixed, like tower-mills, but built of wood. The towers taper and are often octagonal in shape. The name comes from the resemblance to the smocks often worn by farmers in olden times. The most handsome surviving smock-mill is at Cranbrook in Kent.

Not all windmills fit exactly into these categories. There were numerous variations, including one still standing at Chesterton in Warwickshire that was built as an observatory.

Windmill features

There is more to learn about windmills than can be mentioned here, but there are many books to consult if you want to follow

Some windmills have been converted into private houses like this smock-mill near Kingsdown, Kent.

up this topic. And there are a few important things to do if you come across a windmill before you have time for further reading.

First, note the number of sails. Most windmills have four, but in Lincolnshire there are mills with five, six and eight sails. You could try to discover what advantages there were in having more than four sails. While you are about it, notice how the sails work; they are not all alike.

On tower- and smock-mills the sails are fitted to a cap, which protects the tower and the machinery in it. As caps vary in shape and design, it is a good idea to photograph or sketch them and compare them with others in the district, as they often followed a local fashion. If the cap is missing, try to find out what it looked like by asking people or searching local history books.

One of the miller's tasks was to fix the position of the cap – or the main structure of a post-mill – so that it faced the wind. There were many ways of doing this and you should describe the method used in any windmill you study. One of the best ideas was a fantail, usually attached to the cap of a tower- or smock-mill at the side furthest from the sails. This did the work mechanically and automatically. Try to see how it worked and notice the arrangement of the fantail; these often vary between one mill and another. You will probably guess how the fantail got its name.

Most windmills open to the public either have a booklet explaining how the mill worked or a guide to help you.

Looking for vanished windmills

When you search for the site of a demolished windmill, you may expect to find it on a hill where it would catch the wind, but do not be too sure. Some have been moved. I know of a tower-mill that was transported a mile to the opposite end of a village when its original site was needed for a new hospital. The lower portion of this mill is now used as a farm shed, a fairly common use for old mills. Other mills have been turned into private houses, often charming in spite of their odd shape.

Field names again can help your search. Windmill Hill or Windmill Lane may indicate the position of old mills. Inn names can also help. One called The Windmill stands close to the site of a former mill near my home.

Remember also to consult local directories for information about windmills. Those published in the nineteenth century are likely to name the local miller. If you glance through several directories until you can no longer find mention of a miller, you have a rough idea when the mill stopped working. You could also ask around the neighbourhood. Village people often have long memories.

Unusual mills

Your dictionary will tell you that a mill is a building used for the grinding of corn. But the word came to be used more widely to include any industrial building using power. Some windmills in low-lying areas, such as the Fens, were used to drain the land. These were later replaced by mechanical pumping engines housed in remote brick pumping-houses. If you live near the Fens, you could do a fascinating project on the development of pumping methods and the various buildings which have stood on these sites since the land was first drained.

Only a few tide-mills survive. This one at Pembroke was burnt down not long after this photograph was taken but another fine example still stands near Carew Castle.

Once there were tide-mills on most river estuaries. Few remain, but there are fine ones at Woodbridge in Suffolk and near Carew Castle, Pembrokeshire (see picture on page 37). They were water-mills that used the power of the ebbing tide, but as the tide ebbs (or 'goes out') for no more than twelve hours a day, and about forty-five minutes later each day, such mills were inconvenient to work.

You may still find a water-mill that is called 'the fulling mill' because it was used for thickening and cleansing cloth in the Middle Ages when the cloth trade was the country's main industry. At first fulling was done by people called 'walkers' who trampled barefooted on the cloth in long troughs of water mixed with fuller's earth, soap and other ingredients. Later a mechanical hammer operated by a water-wheel was introduced.

Derby has a Full Street and Walker Lane, close together by the river, which is a possible clue to the position of an old fulling mill. Names like Tenter Field or Tenter Lane probably indicate places where the cloth was stretched out and pegged down by tent-hooks to dry after fulling. We still speak of a nervously excited person as being 'on tenterhooks'. Many expressions first used in industry are now part of our language. You might be able to collect some others.

Ruined eighteenth-century post-mill, South Normanton, Derbyshire. The main post could be turned so the sails caught the wind.

Later mills

5

The first silk and cotton mills

Fire risks

Reducing the dangers

Some features to look for

Textile and hosiery mills

The type of mill familiar to you may be the textile or hosiery mill, where cotton goods, lace, silk and many other materials are woven and made up into clothes. The oldest of these mills are likely to be situated alongside fast-flowing rivers or streams. The Stroud Valley in Gloucestershire for example, and the Derwent Valley in Derbyshire have numerous mills on the water's edge. Why do you think this is?

It was on an island in the Derwent at Derby that the first modern mill was built in about 1720. Before then most textile and hosiery work had been done in the workers' homes. The Derby mill was the first in the world where a bell rang at fixed times to summon employees to work and send them home again. It was the first place where the pace of production was fixed by power-driven machinery instead of by the workers; it was the beginning of the process that we now call mass-production.

The mill was used for 'silk throwing', that is for spinning silk thread. It remained a silk mill for 150 years, but most of it was demolished after a fire about sixty years ago. In the eighteenth century it attracted many visitors, and some wrote about what they saw. There is a short but amusing account in *A Tour Through England and Wales* by Daniel Defoe, the author of *Robinson Crusoe*. You might like to read Defoe's account and others, to find out about this mill that was then regarded as an engineering marvel.

England's first factory, the Derby Silk Mill, was on an island in the River Derwent, reached via the bridge in the foreground. The mill had a bell tower exactly like the one in the picture.

In fact people in the eighteenth and early nineteenth centuries were thrilled by the new industrial buildings and the wonderful machinery inside them. Some artists of that period expressed that excitement and enthusiasm in their pictures, as you will see from the splendid illustrations in *Art and the Industrial Revolution* by Francis D. Klingender.

Arkwright's mill

Although it was so successful the Derby mill did not set a fashion in mill building, and it was about fifty years before Richard Arkwright built the first water-operated cotton mill in 1771. This was at Cromford, a few miles further up the same river. It is now used as a colour works. Another one he built slightly later and a short distance away is still used in the cotton industry. Looking at the pictures here and on page 42 you will notice how they differ in appearance. The earlier one is built of stone; the later of brick, which is surprising in a district where building stone is plentiful. The earlier one is a grim fortress of a structure; the other light and cheerful with lots of windows, including arched ones called Venetian windows that are unusual in industrial buildings. Books on architecture will tell you more about them, and will help you look for others. Many mills built between about 1760 and 1830 look most attractive to many people.

The first water-powered cotton mill was built on this site at Cromford, Derbyshire, in 1771. The fortress-like building on the left was probably added slightly later.

Arkwright's Masson Mill, Cromford. Notice the white stone quoins on the corners and the arched Venetian windows. The date 1769 refers to the founding of the firm, not to the building, which was erected in 1783.

Iron-framed mills

Though the early textile mills were built of brick or stone, their floors, staircases and window frames were usually timber. Consequently, they burnt fiercely when fire broke out, as it often did. If you read the records of such mills in your county records office, or in the files of old newspapers in the library, you will notice many accounts of fires. Quite often a mill was burnt down, rebuilt and burnt down again within a few years.

These fires often started when the paraffin lamps or candles that supplied the lighting were knocked over on to such highly inflammable material as cotton waste.

Mill owners insured their premises, but the cost of insurance premiums rose steeply as more fires occurred, just as motor car insurance premiums rise nowadays because there are more accidents. Insurance companies had their own fire brigades then and put metal plates, inscribed with the name or trade-mark of their company, high up on the walls of buildings so that their firemen would not waste energy on buildings insured with rival companies. A few plates remain and are worth noting.

Gas lighting, introduced at the Soho Works in 1802, and electricity, much later, reduced fire risks considerably, but a big step forward had already been taken with the building of the first iron-framed mills. These had brick floors supported by cast-iron beams and columns. Some even had cast-iron window frames. The earliest surviving iron-framed mill is at Shrewsbury. It was built as a flax mill in 1797.

Later mills

With the fire risk reduced by the use of iron in building, it became safer to build taller mills, and it was cheaper too because they used up less land. But many of the mills built after about 1830 seem to us less attractive than the earlier ones. You might discuss this with your friends. Some of them may ask if it matters how a building looks so long as it makes money and keeps people working. What would you say to that?

Even some of the less attractive buildings had interesting features, like cupolas or large clocks. Some mills were even built to look like castles or stately mansions.

You might look round your area and record any interesting mills. Try to guess the date of the buildings and then check in the library. You may even find the date of a building set in the brick or stone above the main entrance.

Tenement mills

Some large mills were built to house many small firms. These were called tenement mills. If there were any in your town, you should be able to find from directories who rented the various sections of the buildings.

Modern mills

Modern mills usually look brighter and cleaner than earlier ones. They often have large windows, and sometimes their surroundings are 'landscaped'; that is, trees are planted and lawns laid out round them to give a pleasing appearance. You might ask yourself if you would rather work in one of these newer buildings or in an older one.

Cressbrook Mill, on the river Wye, Derbyshire, built in 1815. Notice the clock and the triangular stonework over the front of the building, called a pediment.

Machinery, power and processes

6

Knitting machines

Small workshops

Horse and steam power

Furnaces and kilns

It can be fascinating to watch machinery at work in industrial buildings. The people who work the machines are often pleased to talk about them, and if you are handy you will have a marvellous time making models of some of the machinery you see. If you study mechanical drawing (sometimes called engineering drawing) you will find plenty of machines to measure and draw. However complicated they look, they are all based on a few simple processes.

Knitting machines

Some of the most complicated machines are used in the hosiery industry for making such articles as stockings, vests and gloves. Yet most are based on a machine invented in 1589, the year after the defeat of the Spanish Armada.

Before then all stockings were knitted by hand. One Nottinghamshire girl who earned a living by knitting stockings, caught the eye of a clergyman named William Lee, but she refused to go out with him because she said she was too busy. So he set to work to invent a machine that would do the job more quickly – and succeeded. By that time, however, he had lost interest in the girl. Lee was unlucky in another way. His machine did not come into general use for many years; in fact not until about 1670, long after his death.

Many machines based on Lee's invention can be found in museums, especially in the East Midlands, which became the centre of the industry. A few are still in use in factories.

Small workshops

Before the late eighteenth century most of the 'framework knitting' machines, as they were called, were installed in the workers' cottages, usually in upstairs rooms to catch the light. For that same reason, most of the rooms had long windows. Cottages with these long, upstairs windows can still be found in many parts of the country, for example in Devon, in East London and in Nottinghamshire.

Sometimes the machines were worked in specially built small workshops in backyards. You may find one in your home town. If you do, you will notice that it also has long windows to catch the light.

Some other trades were once carried on in small workshops too. Before the days of the motor car almost every village had its smithy where the blacksmith made shoes for horses. Now only a few are used for that purpose, but you might keep a look-out for smithies that have been converted to other uses.

Nail-making was another trade carried out in small workshops. A few of these are still in use in the Staffordshire Black Country, but only a solitary one still remains standing at Belper in Derbyshire, which was a centre of the industry 150 years ago. No nails are made there now.

Horse power

The power needed in these little workshops was usually supplied by the hands or the feet of the workers themselves; other industries, as we have seen in chapter 5, used water or wind, but quite often horses were used.

Flood water, and sometimes coal itself, was brought out of mines by means of a 'horse-gin'. This was a kind of wheel with a beam, attached to which a horse (sometimes an ox or donkey) walked round a circular track. Buckets or 'corves' (baskets), secured by a rope to the gin, were hauled up by the power of the horse operating the gin. You may occasionally come across a circular building, in a farmyard perhaps, which once housed a gin, but usually the only trace left is in a field-name like Gin Field.

Richard Arkwright used horses to drive the cotton machinery in his mill at Nottingham even after he had set up his water-powered mill at Cromford (see chapter 5).

Steam power

The power of horse, water or wind could be effective for driving many forms of machinery, but something more powerful was needed to pump water out of mines. In 1698 a man named Thomas Savery took out a patent for what he called 'The Miner's Friend'. It was a steam engine.

Unfortunately, Savery's engine had many faults, one of which was the risk of its boiler exploding. Then in 1708 a blacksmith named Thomas Newcomen invented an improved form of steam engine. But even this had one important defect. It used a great amount of coal to heat the cylinder. This made it too expensive to be much use except in coal mines, where the fuel was, of course, easy to get.

No Savery engine has survived, but one of Newcomen's still stands in its original engine house at Elsecar near Sheffield. Another that was once used for pumping water for the Coventry Canal, now stands in Newcomen's native town of Dartmouth close to the site of his workshop. Several more are in museums.

In the Science Museum in London is a boiler for a steam engine of the type made by Newcomen. It stood for many years filling a gap in a Derbyshire hedge before anyone recognized it as being what was called a 'haystack' boiler. (If you look at the picture on page 48 you will see why it was given that name.) Eventually it was noticed by an engineer and sent by lorry to the Science Museum. Other haystack boilers may be lying around, or perhaps being used as water tanks. If you are observant you might come across one, or some other interesting industrial relic. If you think you have found one tell one of your teachers or the local museum curator.

The object puzzling this boy is a 'haystack' boiler of an eighteenth century pumping engine used in a colliery at Denby, Derbyshire, now in the Science Museum, London.

Watt's engine

James Watt did not invent the steam engine, but he improved greatly on the work of Savery and Newcomen. He took out a patent for a new separate 'condenser engine' in 1769, but he had to wait six more years to find craftsmen skilful enough to do the precision work he required. Then he solved his problem by going into partnership with Matthew Boulton at the Soho Works, Birmingham.

Watt's engine was a beam-engine, as were nearly all those built before 1850 and quite a number later. Some are still in use. As already mentioned in chapter 3, many engine houses still stand, even if the engines are no longer there, and they are well worth looking out for and photographing or sketching.

There are several good books that explain fairly simply the workings of these various types of steam engines. Make sure also that you understand the meaning of a 'patent'.

Coke-burning

About the time that Newcomen was perfecting his first steam engine, a man named Abraham Darby made an equally important discovery. He found a way of smelting iron by using coke to heat it, and so made possible the large-scale production of iron. Before then charcoal had been used, and it had two great drawbacks. Because of lack of heat, it produced only a poor quality iron, and that only in small quantities. Second, as charcoal is partly-burnt wood, many trees had to be cut down to make it; at a time when many more were being felled to build the wooden ships needed then. Timber was also urgently needed for house building, furniture and pit-props, so there would soon have been a serious shortage of both trees and fuel if Darby had not made his discovery. A similar shortage of fuel may well develop during your lifetime unless we can find a new source of power. You might like to discuss the reasons for this and what could be done about it.

Darby's furnace

Darby's first successful coke-burning furnace can still be seen at Coalbrookdale in Shropshire, where it was built in 1658. Nearly seventy years after it had been converted to burn coke it was enlarged to smelt some of the iron for the first iron bridge in the world. This spans the River Severn in the large village that took its name from the bridge. Some time after the bridge was opened in 1779 the furnace ceased to be used, and gradually came to be buried under slag and rubbish. It has now been unearthed and is an exhibit – like the bridge itself – in the Ironbridge Gorge Museum, which was opened in 1973 and is one of the most interesting industrial museums in Britain.

Wrought iron

That great bridge was made of 'cast iron' smelted in a 'blast furnace'. Cast iron could be reheated in a 'finery' to produce wrought iron, which was stronger and yet could be more easily rolled into various shapes. Ornamental gates, like those which face Buckingham Palace, are often made of wrought iron. Look out for other examples.

The world's first iron bridge spans the river Severn at Iron-bridge, Shropshire. It was cast in Abraham Darby's works at Coal-brookdale nearby.

Before 1784 charcoal was needed to produce wrought iron. Then Henry Cort invented the 'puddling' process that made it possible to use coal as a fuel in a 'reverbatory' furnace. Traces of his ironworks can still be seen at Fareham in Hampshire. Southern England had many ironworks before the inventions of Darby and Cort. If you draw a map of the main iron- and steel-making centres today you will notice that they are now farther north. You should be able to work out the reasons for this, perhaps looking back at chapter 3 to refresh your memory.

Steel-making

Not much wrought iron is produced now. Steel has replaced it. But before 1750 steel-making was just a small part of the iron industry. Benjamin Huntsman took the first important step forward in steel-making techniques when he invented the 'crucible' method, using coal as a fuel. You can see how this method worked at Abbeydale, where it continued in use into this century.

Unfortunately, Huntsman's process produced only small amounts of good steel. A century passed before Bessemer invented his 'converter' and Siemans his 'open hearth' process and made it possible to turn out large amounts of high-grade steel. If you visit a steel works you should remember to ask how its furnaces are heated now.

Other early furnaces

Old lead-mining furnaces were called 'boles', and usually

Coke-fired steel-melting furnaces and crucibles at Abbeydale Industrial Hamlet, Sheffield. They were in use up to the Second World War.

stood on the west side of a hill where they caught the wind to create a draught. Few, if any, boles have survived, but the name Bole Hill often appears on maps of lead-mining districts and tells where these early furnaces stood.

A number of early coke-burning iron furnaces still stand, however, like the two shown in the picture opposite, though sometimes in a ruined state so that they are not easily recognizable. But if you do come across any, they are worth recording and reporting.

Lime kilns

Old lime kilns look rather like furnaces. In these kilns, lime was burnt to a powder to make cement, or for use as a flux in blast furnaces, or for spreading on fields to improve crops on sandy soils. Old lime kilns stand by the harbours in the neighbouring Northumberland seaside villages of Seahouses and Beadnell and at Clovelly in Devon, and are now used to store fishing gear.

Pottery kilns

The kilns in which china clay was baked for the making of

Flint-mill furnaces and flints in a Staffordshire flint-mill.

pottery were quite distinctive in appearance. Many have been pulled down in recent years so it would be well worthwhile to take down the details of any you come across.

In fact industry has changed so rapidly over the last twenty years or so that your records of industrial buildings and their contents could be of great historical value in a few years from now.

Old iron furnaces.

7 People in industrial buildings

People and working conditions

Apprentices

Improving conditions

Industrial housing

People are important but much of the work that used to be done by people is now done by machinery. Your grandfather and his friends may be able to supply a long list of jobs which used to be done by hand but are now done by automation. But even the machines have to be maintained by people. So people are still important.

We can take this a stage further and say that industry is run for the benefit of people. This is something we need to remember. We hear about new factories, new machinery and about what is called 'the national economy'. We need to remind ourselves occasionally that the buildings are there to house the machinery that is producing goods for us. The national economy is simply what we buy and sell. Just as water-mills were built to supply our ancestors with bread, so an aircraft factory is built to supply us with aircraft. If we stopped buying bread or aircraft the mills and factories would have to close.

Working conditions

If industrial buildings are for people it seems fair to expect people who work in them to have reasonable working conditions. Most people would agree today, and so would have most people a hundred years ago. Yet conditions then were desperately bad. You might ask why this was. Did people care less then or is it simply that what one generation considers reasonable is not good enough for the next generation? Again, you could discuss this with your grandfather and his friends. You might ask if conditions have improved since they first started work. On works visits you could ask yourself – and your friends – what improvements you would like to see made in factory life.

Apprenticeships in the past

You might be interested to compare the conditions of an apprentice today with those of the past. Old apprenticeship indentures – legal documents, often on parchment, which had to be signed and witnessed – are fairly easy to find. Many people have them locked away in drawers as curios and you may know somebody who will show you one. The local history library or records office will almost certainly have some you can look at and copy.

An indenture of 1740 says of a fourteen-year-old apprentice wheelwright: 'Taverns, Inns or Ale-houses he shall not haunt. At Cards, Dice, Tables, or any other unlawful game he shall not play.'

Fourteen was then quite old to start an apprenticeship. William Hutton was seven when he began his seven-year apprenticeship at Derby Silk mill shortly after it opened. He was so small that he had to have special shoes called pattens made to fit over his ordinary shoes so that he could reach the machines.

Some apprentices were even younger. Robert Owen, a factory owner, said that many were employed at four or five, and that he had heard of a three-year-old working. These young children were often employed 'to pick up waste cotton from the floor; to go under the machines, where bigger people cannot creep, and the smaller they are the more conveniently they can go under the machines'.

Type of apprenticeship

There were two kinds of apprenticeship in those days:

(a) children living at home with parents or in the home of their employers;

(b) pauper children living in an apprentice house.

The entrance to the apprentice house at Cressbrook Mill, Derbyshire. Built about 1785, it housed the young apprentices, many from London. It has been converted into a row of cottages.

Apprentice houses

Apprentice houses were boarding houses built for children who worked in the mill. These children were nearly always paupers, which means that their parents were either dead or too poor to support them.

In towns, where local children could be employed, there was no need for apprentice houses, but some still stand near country mills. This one is opposite the mill at Cressbrook (mentioned in chapter 5). It has now been converted into a row of cottages, but its original entrance, looking like the front of a church, is unaltered, as you can see.

The children were entirely at the mercy of their masters. Those at Cressbrook were treated quite well, but at Litton Mill, two miles away, and at Lowdham Mill in Nottinghamshire, they had a bad time according to a man named Robert Blincoe, who later wrote an account of his unhappy experiences there.

Children who lived at home were more fortunate. William Hutton hated the mill, but at least he could enjoy some sort of home life outside working hours, and there were occasional days off when there was not enough water to turn the mill-wheel to drive the machinery.

Finding out about conditions

You will naturally want to know what conditions were like in your local mills. Your librarian or county records officer will be able to tell you what accounts have been written about them. Some may be just short diaries or journals, or scattered references in local history books. If you are very lucky you may be able to tape interviews with people who can say, 'My grandfather told me . . .'.

The reports of various commissions of enquiry into the conditions of children in industry are valuable sources of information.

Here are a few to look for:

- Report on Children in Manufactories, 1816 (Peel's Committee)
- Report on Parish Apprentices, 1815
- Report of Committee on Artisans and Machinery, 1824
- Report of Sadler's Committee, 1832
- Report of Commission on Conditions of Children in Mines, 1842

Improvements

The 1833 Factory Act was the first to improve conditions. This Act applied to all textile mills (except silk mills). Children between nine and thirteen were not to work more than nine hours a day (or forty-eight hours a week), of which two hours daily had to be devoted to education. Young people between thirteen and eighteen were limited to a twelve-hour day.

Other Factory Acts reduced hours still further. Most important was the 1850 Act, cutting the hours of adults to ten and a half a day. If you look at the local newspaper files and read of the debates in Parliament before the Acts were passed, you may be surprised at some of the objections that were raised against shorter hours.

The men behind the improvements

Improvements came slowly, but they would have been slower still but for the efforts of a few dedicated men, like Lord Shaftesbury, Michael Sadler, Richard Oastler and Robert Owen, who drew attention to the dreadful state of affairs. You can find out more about these men by looking in the *Dictionary of National Biography*, which you will find in any large library. It consists of many separate volumes, arranged alphabetically, and gives life-stories of famous British people.

Robert Owen

Robert Owen was one of the most remarkable of these men. He cut working hours at his mill at New Lanark at a time when most owners were against this because they feared it would cut their profits. He also introduced unemployment pay and started a sick club and a savings bank. Because he believed that

Cottages in North Street, Cromford, built about 1800 for the workers in Arkwright's cotton mills. The school at the end of the road was built at the same time and is still used.

improved education was essential, he opened what he called an Institution for the Formation of Character. It was an early example of what today we should probably call a community centre. By day there were classes for children over a year old, in the evenings there were lectures and other activities for workers of all ages.

Housing

At New Lanark in Scotland, in 1785, 170 stone houses were built for workers by David Dale, Owen's father-in-law, who then owned the mills. They were good houses by the standards of those days, and are still standing.

Many similar workers' houses are still occupied today. The picture opposite shows North Street, Cromford. Notice the width of the road. The building facing the end of the road is a school which is still used. It is a handsome building which catches the eye immediately, as it was intended to do. This is good early-Industrial Revolution building, as is this housing in Long Row, Belper (below).

The workers' houses in Long Row, Belper, near Cromford, were put up by the Strutt family in the 1790s for their employees in the nearby cotton mill. They are still lived in.

There may be houses in your town or village that were built around this time – roughly 1800 – for mill workers. You would find a visit to one most useful and perhaps somebody living there would let you take photographs.

Modernized colliery (Pye Hill No 2) Nottinghamshire. The headstocks for winding up men and coal are almost entirely encased in concrete. The offices have large windows and young shrubs and trees have been planted to make the area more attractive.

People in industrial buildings today

8

New industrial villages

How improvements have come about

Safety in industrial buildings

The future

Model villages

Nowadays new villages have to be built where a works has been opened a long way from existing houses. These are often spoken of as 'model villages' because their layout is carefully planned by experts. The houses are often built in a series of rectangles, or in a semi-circle round some focal point such as a church, or a parade of shops, or a large green.

Some of these villages are pleasing to look at, but others tend to be rather uninteresting. Can you think of reasons for this monotony? It could be that because the houses were built at much the same time they look alike, whereas most villages look more attractive because the buildings vary in age and style.

Sometimes there are not enough shops, and a shortage of places of amusement for young people. You might like to draw up your own plans for a model village. Consider what people need: shops, a village hall for entertainment, a swimming bath and sports grounds – what else? Compare your plans with those of an existing model village.

Collieries – then and now

If you read the first few chapters of *Sons and Lovers* by D. H. Lawrence, you will have a good idea of how miners lived and worked about sixty years ago. Then they would come home weary and black and have nowhere to wash but a zinc bath in front of the living-room fire. Today a miner may drive to work

Corner of Bolsover Model Village, Derbyshire, built early this century around a spacious, tree-lined green.

in his car, change into overalls, and then, after his shift below, have a hot bath, change his clothes, have a meal in the canteen and drive home again. Life is still hard and dangerous for the miner, but the newer collieries are better designed, pleasanter to look at and more comfortable to work in than the older ones.

Trade unions

You could consider how these improvements in the mines and other industrial buildings have come about. The trade unions have undoubtedly played an important part. This is a vast subject, but you should find out as much as you can about the work of the unions, both in the country as a whole and in your area. Study in your local history library should tell you if your own district has seen many strikes in the past. If there seem to have been a large number, try to find out why. It could have been because of problems in a particular industry or in just one factory.

Strife by John Galsworthy is a good play about strikes that you might like to read and then discuss.

Some improvements have been brought about because people

have demanded them. In a country like ours, where people are able to say and write very much what they please, changes can be made if enough people want changes.

Often public opinion is first aroused by writers. Authors like Charles Dickens, George Eliot (a woman writing under a man's name), H. G. Wells, George Orwell and others have drawn attention to conditions that should be improved. Members of Parliament have followed up these suggestions, and new laws have been passed to right old wrongs.

Improving industrial relations

You may have heard lately about new methods of working that are being tried in some factories. More than one firm now allows the workers to choose their own starting and finishing times, providing they work an agreed number of hours in the week. This method is called 'Flexitime'. Some firms are trying to find more varied and interesting ways of doing jobs. Others are giving more information to the men on the shop floor about

Industrial grime in Sheffield. A nineteenth-century building is in the foreground; later ones in the background.

the jobs they are doing and about work to be done in the future. In a number of firms the manual workers on the workshop floor have a representative on the board of management. All these are attempts to improve what is called 'labour relations' – in other words, to see that management and manual workers get on better together and that working conditions are improved. Sometimes this is successful; sometimes not.

New Factory Acts

We have already discussed the early Factory Acts, but new ones are passed frequently. Some make slight alterations that are hardly noticed outside a particular industry; others make quite dramatic changes. On your works visits keep an eye open for regulations concerned with the Factory Acts. They will usually be posted up on walls inside the buildings. Fairly regularly Factory Inspectors come round to see that the Acts are being obeyed.

Safety in industrial buildings

In particular you should look out for safety regulations. For

Old and new industrial buildings in Sheffield. Which would you rather work in?

instance, every works where electrical gear is used must display notices about the treatment of people suffering from electric shocks. You will find them on the walls of garages, amongst other places.

Many accidents occur in industry. Some are only slight, and so may not be reported in newspapers. On the other hand, strikes are nearly always reported. Yet far more working hours are lost through accidents than because of strikes.

You can check that for yourself. Reports on the numbers of accidents at work are issued regularly by Her Majesty's Inspectors of Factories. These are usually reported briefly in some newspapers, but the full reports are published as pamphlets by Her Majesty's Stationery Office (usually shortened to HMSO). These can often be bought from a local bookseller, and the more important ones may be in your local library.

It might be useful to consider the causes of accidents. Many happen through sheer carelessness, hurrying and neglecting proper precautions. And accidents can be caused by long hair getting caught in machines.

Workmen become so used to their jobs that they rarely worry about possible accidents. Most of the worrying is done by their relatives. In *Sons and Lovers*, Lawrence describes the feelings of a wife whose husband is hurt in a coal mine. A colliery disaster is well described by A. J. Cronin in *The Stars Look Down*. You could try in poetry or prose to imagine how it feels to have a husband or father engaged in dangerous work.

You could find out which industries have the most accidents. To get an accurate impression you should know the number of people employed in the industry. You could perhaps convert your results into a graph.

The future

Some firms offer money prizes for suggestions that will reduce risks of accidents. On works visits you should look out for additional safety precautions that could be suggested. Sometimes, too, prizes are offered for ideas for improving methods of work. When you start work you should keep your eyes open for chances of this sort. In fact this project on industrial buildings should not end when you hand it in to be assessed. It could go on all your life.

We have seen many improvements, but there are many more to be made. Twenty years ago Sheffield and Stoke-on-Trent were smoky cities. Today the air there is clear of smoke. But too much smoke still hangs over other places, and there is still too much industrial pollution of other kinds. If you fish, you will know how much harm is done to rivers by industrial waste.

Too much industrial waste still lies around in the countryside. Much derelict land has been tidied up and converted to other uses, but there is a great deal more to be done. At the same time, there are many industrial relics that are worth finding and saving because they tell us so much about our past. Just what is to be preserved is up to you and your generation to decide.

The clean face of modern industry. Iron foundry at Belper, Derbyshire, built in 1949.

How to find out more 9

Museums

The Science Museum, Exhibition Road, South Kensington, London SW7 2DD.
York Castle Museum, Tower Street, York.
Abbeydale Industrial Hamlet, Abbeydale Road South, Sheffield.
Shepherd Wheel, Whiteley Wood, Sheffield (this is a preserved water-powered grinding shop).
North of England Open-Air Museum, Beamish Hall, County Durham.
Ironbridge Gorge Museum, Telford, Shropshire (this includes the Blists Hill Open-Air Museum, Coalport Road, Madeley, Telford, Shropshire).
Museum of Science and Engineering, Exhibition Park, Great North Road, Newcastle-upon-Tyne.
Welsh Folk Museum, St Fagans, Cardiff, Glamorgan.
Avoncroft Museum of Buildings, Stoke Prior, Bromsgrove, Worcestershire.
Llechwedd Slate Caverns, Blaenau Festiniog, Merionethshire (disused slate mine where you can go underground to see how slate was extracted and split).
Industrial Museum, Moorside Mills, Eccleshall, Bradford, Yorkshire.

This is only a small selection of museums of industrial interest. To find others, and for information about opening times, you should consult the following:

Museums and Galleries in Great Britain and Ireland (ABC Travel Guide, published each year).

AA Britain's Heritage (Letts, published each year).

Maps

You will find the Ordnance Survey map of your district helpful when looking for industrial buildings. The 1 inch to 1 mile scale is the most suitable for your purpose.

The local search series

Editor: Mrs Molly Harrison MBE, FRSA

This book is one of a highly successful series designed to help young people to look inquiringly and critically at particular aspects of the world about them. It encourages them to think for themselves, to seek first-hand information from other people, to make the most of visits to interesting places, and to record their discoveries and their experiences.
Many boys and girls enjoy detective work of this kind and find it fun to look for evidence and to illustrate their findings in ways that appeal to them. Such lively activities are equally rewarding whether carried out individually or in a group.

Already published

The English Village
Dennis R. Mills

Under the editorship of Molly Harrison

The English Home
Molly Harrison

The Public Library
Frank Atkinson

Living Creatures of an English Home
Olive Royston

The Public Park
Herbert L. Edlin

Farms and Farming
Rowland W. Purton

The Post Office
Olive Royston

Looking at the Countryside
Annesley Voysey

A Home of Your Own
Margaret Kirby

The Theatre
Olive Ordish

Graves and Graveyards
Kenneth Lindley

Rivers and Canals
Rowland W. Purton

Museums and Galleries
Molly Harrison

Markets and Fairs
Rowland W. Purton

Trees and Timbers
Herbert L. Edlin

Dress and Fashion
Olive Ordish

Looking at Language
J. A. Robinson

Factories, Forges and Foundries
Roy Christian

Forthcoming

The Town Hall
Olive Royston

Seaside and Seacoast
Kenneth Lindley

Collecting Out of Doors
Joan Rendell